ACTING

Musings from 40 years on the stage

2

ACTING

Musings from 40 years on the stage

By Gerald Drake with John Middleton

To my wife of 50 years Kathie (who agreed if we made it through the 60s we'd be OK) my daughter Kelly, son Bobby and daughter Kris and her husband Mickey and my grandson Leo, I dedicate this book.

Cover photo, Gerald Drake as King Arthur in KING ARTHUR AND THE MAGIC SWORD, 1966, photo by C.T. Harwell

CONTENTS

FOREWARD

Life is experience. – Joseph Campbell

I've experienced many things in my life, but with no one to share the experience with, what does it become, but a hollow crown?

BEING AN ACTOR

An actor can be more real onstage than in real life.

Nothing is harder than telling the truth. In real life, I weigh my every action and its consequences. But in the theater, I hide behind a character, and I can do anything.

The theater makes me feel truly alive. In a world of passive entertainment, where our emotions are experienced vicariously through TV and movies, the theater demands some kind of reaction, some kind of response. As actor and as audience, all my senses are working.

I love the theater, always have and always will. When I come to the theater, I feel I am coming home. I feel safe. I feel safer in the theater than I do in my life. Maybe because I know how everything will turn out, as opposed to life, the great mystery!

INFLUENCES

People write books about going to the theater and seeing a certain show or a certain performance and how it changed their lives. That happened to me at the Children's Theatre Company in 1967.

It was the final performance of *Hang Onto Your Head*. I sat in the front row with my wife Kathie and I wept. The level of artistry, the story-telling, the love! I had never had an experience like that before in my life.

A ran backstage. (At that time, the theater was in a museum, so backstage was a gallery of Chinese art just off of stage right.) I told the director I had to work with him. That spring, he cast me as Johnny Appleseed. That summer, he asked me to join the company.

I've never had another moment in the theater quite like that one. I wonder, is it like "being saved?" Can it only happen once?

In any event, that experience is why I'm here.

You, also, will affect people and learn how extraordinary that is.

Welcome to the kingdom of art!

SACRED SPACES

When you were a child, did you have a special place where you went to play? Maybe it was a place your Mom worried about you going to, a place maybe only you knew about. That place where you played as a child was a sacred space. You made it that way. We need sacred spaces. So you created one, or several, with your imagination and concentration, through your desire for a sacred space.

I have a book called *The Dictionary of Imaginary Places*. Neverland is in it, and Wonderland, and many others. These are all sacred spaces where we can be, and do, and create worlds. As we get older we continue to look for sacred spaces in our lives.

In the theater, we find sacred spaces where we rehearse our work and where we perform for others. These are the descendants of the sacred spaces we cherished as kids. They have that same power and that same capacity to let us play, and carry on, and freely explore the wonders of the world.

When you are here in this space it should feel special. Some spaces simply are sacred – you know it the moment you enter them. But other places need us to make it special. We make them sacred by the way we treat them.

The theater is sacred, declared holy by us, the actors. And a sacred space demands respect, for we are coming together to create art, a living art, with all that implies: discipline, reverence, concentration, focus, imagination, celebration, the need to express something true, and the love of the opportunity to do it.

There is much energy here in the space I have known for over forty years. Here at the Children's Theatre Company, hundreds of plays have been performed on this stage, thousands of performances, involving hundreds of actors. It is magical! The energy and wonderment of young actors, eager to learn and commit to the work. The mentors surrounding them, being a positive influence. All performing for children, their parents and grandparents, a community. What could be better than that?

AUDITIONING

The hardest part about auditioning is just showing up. If you can do that, leap! And all will be well.

When I first auditioned at CTC, I stood outside the door of the theater. After a moment I turned around, said, "I can't," and started to walk away. A young boy came up to me, Neil Danahy, and said, "Don't go, they need men." I looked down at him and said "Okay."

For my audition, I read a speech in which King Arthur says, "...if I run I will never be king." And in that moment, somehow I was able to open myself up. The fear and frustration I was feeling as an actor become the fear and frustration of the character and that line, "if I run I will never be king," came straight from my heart. "Yes! This is my moment, I cannot run!"

After I finished the director smiled and said, "The part is yours. We would very much like you to be King Arthur." I was nineteen years old, I hadn't been in a play in months, and now I was offered the lead in *King Arthur and the Magic Sword*.

I got in my car and drove to my fiancée's house and jumped up and down in the living room saying, "I'm in a play! I'm in a play!" My 95-year-old mother-in-law still remembers that moment.

So you see? You never know.

All you can do is make your offering. If they don't see it, well, that's too bad for them.

Audition. Share something of yourself. If you love the theater it will show. And if you've offered your gift, you've already won.

REHEARSALS

Rehearsals should have a sense of play.

Remember when you were eight? Remember when you would turn out the lights, crawl under a sheet, turn on a flashlight and scare your brother? That's what I'm talking about.

The rehearsal room should be a place where you gather all the stuff you need to really play. You need your toys, right? I often bring in substitute props and substitute costume pieces. Or maybe it's special lighting, or a little music.

And remember – you were never graded on how well you played. Failure? What failure? Failure has nothing to do with "play."

Let down the façade and get to work, playing. Make choices. Try out different histories for your character, different obstacles, different combinations of actors working together. And always listening, listening, listening! With wide-eyed wonderment.

Yes, wonderment. This is serious play – not running around or jumping up and down – but the focused concentration of serious play in a sacred space. So treat it with respect, like a little child going to church. Listen. Observe.

You were chosen to be here because something was seen. Perhaps some part of yourself that's as yet unknown to you, but waiting to be revealed. You're on a journey of discovery and there are clues everywhere.

IDEAS and CHOICES

The director of *Young Lions* said Montgomery Clift would show up each day with fifty ideas for any given scene. Other actors might have one idea every two days.

More ideas mean more choices. That's what you want. Remember, there are no wrong choices, only better choices. The more choices you have, the more really good ones you might find.

Let's say you're playing Long John Silver in *Treasure Island*. You look at the character – a middle-aged man with a wooden leg who is in charge of pirates. He can't physically master all those men, so he has to use other means to get them to do what he wants. You have an idea: "I must be really good at persuading people to do things." Now what choices will you make? You can choose to bluster, bully, cajole, amuse, seduce, tempt, coax, trick, wheedle, shock, flatter, beg, and on and on.

Start by asking yourself lots of questions. What's happening in this scene? What's the action? What's happening to my character? What is my character thinking? Doing? What does my character want? Need? Where has she been? Where is she going? Does she have a secret? What does she think is going to happen?

And don't be satisfied with the first ideas that come into your head. More ideas mean more choices!

LISTENING

Young actors are forever saying their lines and then they turn toward the audience and wait to say their next line. Listen! Listening is an action. It's choosing not to speak. And like any action, it takes energy. The theater takes tremendous energy.

And don't pretend that you're listening! Really listen. How can you tell the difference? When you're pretending to listen, your concentration is on yourself – "Do I look like I'm listening?" When you're really listening your concentration is on the person speaking. Let their words affect you. How do they make you feel? What images and sensations do they provoke?

When you really listen, you learn things, your responses become more natural and interesting, and you help the audience hear the play.

RESEARCH

You've been cast in a role. Now you have to build a character. How do you do it?

What's your name? The playwright has given you a lot of clues. Sometimes the playwright has given you clues without even knowing it. When asked about a character's name in *The Diviners*, playwright Jim Leonard said it didn't mean anything, he just pulled the name off a billboard. But out of all possible names from all possible sources, he chose that one. Of course it means something.

Go to the dictionary. I go to the dictionary a lot. "Oh, my character is named James Witless?" I go to the dictionary to make sure I know exactly what "witless" means. (Not filled with wit.)

Or you're playing Leontes in The Winter's Tale. Leontes means "the lion." That tells you almost everything you need to know right there.

Beyond the dictionary, there are worlds of research to inspire you: photographs, paintings, movies, documentaries. Study images for the physicality of the people in them. Body language, facial hair, clothes, hairstyles, facial expressions, eyebrows, noses, all the visible signs that reveal the hidden energy within every human.

You contain resources in your own mind. Meditate. Lie back, close your eyes, and let your characters come to you. Ask them to act out the scene. It might be shockingly brilliant. Pose questions to them. Watch and listen to their responses.

Keep going back to the script. The more you understand, the more clues you'll find there. Continue to look for ways to visualize what you are reading and feeling.

And don't stop at feeling! Some actors think that "feeling the moment" is their whole job. If they feel it, they've succeeded. And if they don't, they've failed. You can be acting so hard and feeling it in your bones, but the feeling goes no further than your nose. Why? Because it's not enough to feel things. You have to share what you're feeling with an audience.

Are you not sure how to do this? Go back to your research. Find images that convey something of the feeling you're trying to share and use that to come up with an action that will carry that feeling to an audience.

BUILDING A CHARACTER

Start by focusing on what the scenes are about. It does no good to rehearse over and over if you don't understand what the scene is about. Only when you understand can you make discoveries and make it your own.

If you know what the scene is about you will find many ways of approaching that scene. If you don't know what the scene is about, you're doomed to robotically repeat whatever actions the director has given you. You will begin to respond before the dialogue even suggests it. Your character will not be a living thing, but a copying machine.

Once you have an idea of what each scene is about, start to explore how each scene builds on the last. One thing leads to another.

Now that you have a feeling for the structure of the play, you can begin to figure out how your character fits within that framework. How are you moving the story forward? In *The Prince and the Pauper*, there's a scene early on where the Prince, disguised, goes out of the palace for the first time. The young actor playing the Prince wanted to play the end of the scene – when things go badly – and so he had to be reminded to discover the scene as it unfolded. The scene begins with the thrill of being out on his own, the wonderment of being surrounded by street vendors, selling things. The joy and frustration of the Prince! Bursting to tell others, but he can't. He had to remember to let the story unfold for himself so that it could unfold for the audience.

Let your attention broaden to the actors around you. Much of your character will be revealed by your relationships to the other characters. In our production of *Peter Pan*, I played Smee. The actor playing Captain Hook and I had to discover and (mostly) agree on the relationship between these two. Then, every moment together on stage was about making choices that defined, deepened and revealed that relationship – not a series of bits.

Bits! The longer you've been in the theater the more frustrating cheap acting gets. Bits that get modest laughs or a few chuckles. We don't want chuckles. We want the deep, delighted, grab-your-stomach, bent-over-until-it-hurts laughs.

You're never going to get those laughs unless your character reveals something true. All characters must be grounded in truth. What is the truth of the scene? What are you after? As James Whitmore says, "What are you trying to sell?"

Everything should be done with artistry. Every character demands artistry, even the derelict, the drunkard, the misshapen, the horrifying - all need your artistry. Do you know what I mean? The character needs to be controlled, shaped, molded and spun out by you. You are in control. Active. Not back on your heals but on the balls of your feet.

Bring your artistry, your curiosity, your taste, to your character. Be open to inspiration – you never know where it's going to come from.

Does your costume tell you anything? "Ooh, I wear very tight pants. I must walk this way."

Figure out what you need! When I played *The Miser*, I had so much dialogue, so many words, I tried my best to have my lines memorized before rehearsals began. I didn't want to have to worry about that. I wanted to get the language out of the way for a while and concentrate on the stuff that comes to me when I'm in action.

I might come into rehearsal and say to the director, "I think my character has a limp because he was kicked by a cow." (Some directors are more open to that than others.)

Remember, rehearsals are so you can believe. Performances are so the audience believes.

You can't believe until you understand the play and your role in it. From understanding comes the ideas you use to explore your character and make discoveries. Keep making discoveries. Discover the scene, discover the line, discover the action, and your character will be discovered by the audience.

Good luck.

STAGE MANAGERS

The Stage Manager is the overall supervisor of the stage and actors. A good stage manager runs the rehearsals like a fine watch. If an actor is not needed they are not called. A Stage Manager (SM) is a psychologist for those who are distraught, a doctor for those ill, a guardian for actors against their unseen forces and close friends for those who need counsel.

You ask a SM a question and they have the answer or know where to find it.

Even Hitler loved dogs.

Don't fall into the trap of playing one note. "Oh, this character is mean. I'll be so mean!" Where's the weak spot? What's her sense of humor? People aren't computers. They're complex creatures and require your full exploration to represent them.

Find the positives, the negatives are already in the script.

People were surprised when Anthony Quinn found humor in Stanley Kowalski in *A Streetcar Named Desire*. But of course he did! Finding Stanley's humor makes the moments of horror in that play so much more terrifying.

When I played Long John Silver in *Treasure Island*, a critic chastised me for being too nice. What a stupid thing to say. Too nice!? I murdered a young man by breaking his back with my crutch! I should have called the critic and discussed the performance. Why not?

I kept thinking about Ted Bundy, the serial killer. How obviously dangerous was he? What was he like at the grocery store?

Find the humor if it's serious. Find the danger if it's comic. Find the love in the fights. Find the fear in the love scenes. Otherwise we're just postcards.

25

BEING AN ACTOR IN CHILDREN'S THEATRE

Acting in children's theater can be much more challenging than acting in adult theater. In both, you need to build a character, but look how much you're given by Shakespeare, Moliere, Chekhov, or Tennessee Williams.

Here's Arthur Miller's first description of Willy Loman:
"From the right, Willy Loman, the Salesman, enters, carrying two large sample cases. He is past sixty years of age, dressed quietly. Even as he crosses the stage to the doorway of the house, his exhaustion is apparent. He unlocks the door, comes into the kitchen, and thankfully lets his burden down, feeling the soreness of his palms. A word escapes his lips – it might be "Oh, boy, oh, boy."

Now look at children's theater:
"Once upon a time there was a king and he had a son."

Many characters don't even have names: the Prince, the old woman, the North Wind, a girl, etc. Sometimes they're not even human – a crocodile, a fish, a dog, a kitten – but you still need to make them real.

And the stories we tell! They are sweeping tales of life and death, forgiveness, courage, faith!

I think it's the most challenging work you will ever encounter.

But, oh, the rewards! Only in Children's Theatre can you play a rich toad with a mania for cars, Mark Twain, an old dog who loves Christmas and a White Knight in one year!

I love the stretch, the possibilities, the research. I love the many different worlds to explore, the characters to put on and speak through, the journeys to go on. They say variety is the spice of life. The variety in Children's Theatre is so spicy, the challenge so expansive and delightful, that the sense of play I felt when I was eight years old is back.

What do you want to play today? Cowboys? Army? Knights in armor? Lost in the jungle?

Children's theater is about big stakes, high risks, and life or death situations. Something has to be won, conquered, discovered and it has to be done by 4:00 this afternoon!

Glorious!

ACT ON THE LINE

Act on the line, not in between the lines. Save that for the movies. We "act on the line" in real life. Someone says something and all the while they're talking, we're listening, responding, figuring out what we are going to say next. When they give us an opening, we jump in. We don't pause between each "line."

Sometimes we try so hard to show that we are acting that we forget to respond naturally. That comes from not listening. Listen and respond.

LEARNING LINES

Many actors have developed many techniques for learning lines. I have labored over this for years.

Then I chanced to read a biography of Sir Ralph Richardson. In it, he described his method for memorizing lines. He wrote them out on paper, over and over.

I think there's something valuable in physically writing the words out. Moving the pen across the page. A connection is made between the hand and the brain.

I tried it and it works for me. Maybe it will for you.

Do you have a beautiful voice? You do? Congratulations. But be careful. Some actors become so enamored of their beautiful voices that speaking becomes the whole performance. I guarantee you, no audience member walks out of the theater saying, "I loved her resonance." Or "I adored his diction."

No. Audiences walk out saying things like "I loved when he did that one thing!" "Did you see her do that?" There's no acting without actions. Do things!

When Uta Hagen saw John Barrymore in *Hamlet*, what moved her most was a moment when Barrymore tore his cloak in the bedroom scene with the queen. More than Barrymore's voice or Shakespeare's words, it was an action that thrilled her.

UNDERSTUDYING

If you have been cast as an understudy, your responsibility is to shape your performance to the mold the actor you're understudying has created. As far as possible, you need to match that actor's dynamics and, within this world, find some truth for yourself.

The other actors, the stage manager and technicians have shaped their roles to match the rhythms of the other actor. Don't throw them off with your own interpretation of the role, even if you think it's more correct. That is not your choice.

If possible, talk with the actor about the role. You can learn a lot from this.

And be prepared! I understudied a play in the 80's. I was not prepared. I had to go on. I'll never do that again.

In 2006, I understudied Brian Murray who played the pope in a production of *Edgardo Mine* at the Guthrie. He was in poor health throughout the run of the show. I was told to be ready to go on. I studied the part thoroughly and felt ready. Every day I thought I would be called, but in the end, he did every performance. It was an exhausting and stressful experience, but I was ready!

WHEN A SHOW CLOSES

We held the closing party for *The Velveteen Rabbit* (1988) in the scene shop. We stood around, sipping punch and taking photos. Billy, who provided the voice of the rabbit, was overcome. The end of a show means an end to the close friendships you develop with your cast, the end of the ritual of doing the show, the end of the particular creativity within yourself that the show demands. He felt, keenly, the loss of all of that. Poor Billy.

Over the next few years, Billy did a couple more shows, even touring to Moscow with the company, but it was never the same. Two or three years later, eighteen-year-old Billy came backstage with his girlfriend after a performance of *Cinderella*. "Hey, Jer!" he said to me. "It's me, Billy. How are you? Great show. We should have lunch sometime." We never had lunch. Billy was grown up and had moved on, but I'll never forget him at that cast party.

Some actors let go easily. Some have a much a harder time. Like a graduating class, the actors say, "I'll never forget you! Best friends forever!" But it seldom works out that way, does it? I've stayed in touch with some people. Others have disappeared forever. I've cried when a show closed. I've laughed. I've said, "Thank God that's over!"

All shows close. And when they're gone, there's not much left behind. There are memories, of course, in the minds of the actors and those who saw it. Maybe a few photos, some press clippings, a program. But the performance? It's gone and cannot be repeated.

It's sad. But it's also good. You've created a world, and you've let it go. You've sweat and cried and bled with others and now you part.

Isn't that just what life is like?

Cherish the elusive quality of theater. The grief of saying goodbye to a show you love reminds you that you're alive, loving and growing and devout and holy.

And then you move on.

MENTORS

In the early 1970's, four of us, John Jenkins, his wife Linda, my wife Kathie and I had a job at the Minnesota State Fair. We performed a "sawing a woman in half" routine for the Pioneer Chainsaw Company. Between performances – we did five shows a day – John and I would sit on a bank and talk about the theater.

I had been hired fulltime at the Children's Theatre Company. I felt very lucky. There weren't a lot of fulltime acting jobs in town. I was newly married, so I wasn't going to run off and study in Europe. Best of all, I had been given the opportunity to work with people I admired at a theater I respected.

I joined CTC to watch Bain Boehlke act. He was only six years older than me, but he had studied in Europe, was an Army vet, and now he was my teacher and colleague. I felt that I could learn how to perform and how to develop a character if I spent several years just watching him.

That's what I did. I spent my twenties watching, listening, sometimes crying.

Eventually, I got to the point where I imitated him too well and needed to develop my own style and let my own self through.

It took time, but I did that, too.

Mentors continue to grow and change, too. Bain left CTC when he realized that his passion was driving him away from the large-scale productions of CTC and toward a more intimate theater in a more intimate space. He founded his own theater in an abandoned storefront and was very successful.

If you can, find people that you truly respect, real artists. Sadly, there aren't many around. You're looking for an artist who doesn't apologize for what she believes in, someone who lives the life of an artist. People who've dedicated their lives to their art, sacrificed their relationships with family and friends to do this thing. I don't know if that's good or bad, healthy or unhealthy, but I know the commitment that it takes.

There's no one way of being an artist, of course. You want to find a good match. Someone you resonate with. Someone who shares your aesthetic, who nurtures your creative impulse and will help you grow and be fruitful. If you love watching them, working with them, talking to them, and feel you are learning from them, then by all means grab onto them and take what you can!

What was it like to study with Picasso? What about Orson Welles?

How easy it is to make sweet music when you're in an orchestra surrounded by great musicians! How hard it is to just keep time if you're surrounded by beginners.

Treat these years as an apprenticeship, as a painter, sculptor or musician apprentices with a master. Surround yourself with beauty and great thought. Strive for your truth.

And when you're as good as the master, move on!

ENSEMBLE

I have always been fascinated by the idea of a group of actors working together over a period of time to make something greater than themselves. To be comfortable with each other, trusting, feeling each other's impulses, supporting each other and knowing when one is awry.

This was true of us at the Children's Theatre Company beginning in 1965 and continuing through the years that CTC went from a small, struggling troupe to a highly respected institution with a national reputation and a big, new theater that opened in 1974. We had a real company. Actors, playwrights, musicians, designers, dancers – all working toward a goal: great art!

This is a very difficult thing to maintain; so much is always pulling the organization apart. Large offers of money to actors to do films and other projects. Domineering directors that make actors feel useless when not listened to or considered. Dull personalities that drive artists away.

But when it works, when actors stay together over time, with playwrights writing for them, everyone devoted to the work at hand, what could be more exciting?

Sadly, ensembles are rare and getting rarer.

Most theaters can't afford it. Some actors don't like it. Many directors don't think it's necessary.

Certainly, actors come together and form an ensemble of sorts every time a play is produced. And sometimes, the results are outstanding. But how much more would be possible if the actors stayed together for five years? Ten years?

One play, or even one season, doesn't give the actors the time to come together the way a true ensemble does.

Actors go from theater to theater, auditioning for this show or that, hoping for any job they can get. If cast, there is a lot of pressure on the actor to do his thing – whatever that is. That's what got him the job. So he does his thing and then moves on to the next show and does his thing again. How does he grow? What incentive is there to challenge himself?

But in an ensemble, you don't have to worry about proving yourself every show. You've got the job. Your fellow actors have already seen your thing. Now they're anxious to see you do something else. You have the space and freedom and encouragement you need to try new things, to challenge yourself and grow.

The ensemble will create a way of working. A shorthand will develop. The time-consuming business of learning how to work with your scene partners will have been completed long ago. Instead of the cautious feeling-out of one another that takes up the first few weeks of rehearsal, you can dive right in and get going. More time to create new worlds!

Look at the work created by the great ensembles of the past: Stanislavski's Moscow Arts Theater, Orson Welles' Mercury Theater, Peter Brook's company, Shakespeare's company.

How wonderful to feel yourself a part of a community! Don't you long for that? Many of us don't even know our neighbors any more. Don't you want to be part of a creative community, contributing your talents to something greater than yourself?

I do.

You might not find a company to be a part of, but you can be generous with yourself, with your work, with your compliments and your support. Even if we're not in the same room together, we are all artists. We are all working toward something greater than our individual selves.

Artists should like other artists. No petty bickering please! Be generous to the people you're with, because you're all working together, making art together.

Be joyous!

THE ROLE OF THE DIRECTOR

There are as many different ways to direct a play as there are directors. Some are telling you what to do every second. Some say nothing. Some have you sit around a table for weeks, reading the script over and over. Others get you up on your feet right away.

I suppose any of these ways can work, as long as the director has a vision for the play.

I can tell you what doesn't work. I have seen actors brought to a total standstill by a director. Intimidated, frustrated to the point of tears, losing their sense of relaxation, their imagination, their creative impulse, left standing motionless and miserable, waiting for instructions.

In general, what you and I are looking for in a director is someone who can shape the overall arc of the play and keep all elements working together. Each scene should build on the last. Together, the scenes should build toward a satisfying whole. The costume, set and lighting designs should work together to illuminate the story. And the characters should believably inhabit the same world together.

This seems obvious, but I've seen many plays in which one actor is doing musical comedy, another *Commedia*, another is performing a TV drama and so on. That's the director's fault.

In turn, our responsibility to the director is to go with their vision. If a director asks you to do something that seems off the wall, something you never would have thought of yourself, go with it! So often, those turn out to be the most exciting performances.

You're looking for a director that can help you unlock the mystery of your character. You want a director who helps guide you, supports you, inspires you. Someone who cherishes the creative impulse.

I once had a director say to me that 90% of his job was casting. There is a certain comfort in that. If a thoughtful, imaginative director has cast you in a role, know that there's something about you that is already shaping the role.

Remember, the director doesn't know what it's supposed to be, either. There's a comfort in that, too. Stay fluid with whatever the director offers. Unless, of course, the director is insane, or perfunctory, or dull, or witless, or boring, or uninspiring.

In that case, you're on your own.

CHILD ACTORS

Have you ever watched children at play? They are natural actors. They play seriously, joyfully, with imagination and concentration, fully immersed in the world they've created. We should all strive to bring sense of play to our work.

Unfortunately, most children forget all that as soon as they step on stage. They learn their parts by rote, rattling off their lines in one big rush, not listening to themselves or anyone else.

Break this. Take time with them. They need your patience and your example. Listen to them and respond from your heart. Teach them the "why" of things.

Treat them as colleagues. Inspire them. That's what they want and we should give them credit for it. Be clear. Listen. Share with them your rituals and your view of the theater. They are eager to learn, but need your help. They each have a serious, joyful, imaginative artist inside, waiting to be shown the way out.

I think about those troupes of child actors, a hundred or so years ago, that toured the country, performing Shakespeare. What was that like? I hope they were treated with respect and cherished as they deserved to be.

THE UNSPEAKABLE

I have been in thousands of performances in hundreds of plays, but they're still there: the gremlins. The sprites. Whispering in my ear, "You can't do this."

I pretend I'm fine. But I'm not fine. I can't remember my lines. I can't remember anything!

In those moments, I say a little prayer and tell myself, it's not nerves. It's anticipation! Playing the positives, I tell myself that I can't wait to get out there and tell this story.

Sometimes, I even believe myself.

At any moment on stage the director should be able to say, "Stop!" and a photo could be taken that would show your character, intention, needs, mood, feelings and attitude. Every moment could be a photograph, with your character frozen in time, a picture of a life on stage.

What is your picture saying in this moment? Do we see who you are? Where you've been? Where you're going? What you want? How you relate to the people and objects around you? Or is it an unfocused snapshot of someone just standing there?

This is something to remember.

THE THIRD EYE

You will learn to see yourself on stage with your third eye. With practice, you'll find that you can look around, feel the pulse of the audience, and check in with the other actors. This is information for you to tap into!

A part of you hovers out there with the audience and you watch yourself. You'll see your physicality, your relation to the other actors, and get a sense of the world of the play.

It's amazing.

FAR OUT

I can't tell you how many times I've heard a young actor say to the director, "My character would never do that!"

Long ago, a director once said to me, "Right now, someone, somewhere, is doing something so far out you couldn't possibly even imagine it."

The caveman lurks behind the eyes of every one of us. We mostly keep a lid on it, but it's back there, waiting for the right moment.

If the director asks you to do something that you think is too far out, do it. You'll figure out the why later. Because, come on, what really is too far out? Pick up a newspaper. People are far out.

Why do we get stuck thinking there's only one way to say or do anything? There are as many ways to say "I love you" as there are people on earth.

All dialogue has meaning. No character says something for no reason. Every time you speak you're trying to convince, bribe, seduce, impress, persuade, dominate or control someone else. Maybe you're doing all those things at once.

Speaking is an action! Keep it active. Make a choice. If it doesn't work, make another choice. Then make some more.

I saw a production in which one of the lead actors made one choice. One choice physically. One choice vocally. After thirty seconds, you saw the entire performance which would go on for another two hours. One choice, over and over. It was like being hit in the head with a hammer.

See lots of other plays and the players in them. Get a sense of all the different ways to interpret a role. See the variety that's out there.

If there was only one, "right" way to perform a play or interpret a role, then once that's been done there would be no need to ever do it again. Thankfully, that's not even close to being true.

Keep trying things. In rehearsal, why not make different choices every day? (Some directors get so uptight about this. I don't know why.)

I worked with a director who once had us play each other's parts. I watched as an actor played my role, then I played his. It was very painful at first – my ego was in the frying pan for a while – but once I got past that, there was a lot to learn. I saw the other actor doing things I didn't know I was doing. I saw him doing things I wasn't doing. I thought I knew when my character's pants should fall down (it was a clown role, so, naturally, the pants had to fall down), but suddenly, there were dozens of places for the pants to fall down. I had more choices. There were possibilities for physicality and timing that I would never have known existed.

I can't say I'd want to do this in every rehearsal process, but in this case, it was revelatory.

ENTRANCES AND EXITS

How important they are!

It has been said, and sometimes by me, that a good entrance and a good exit are half the performance. Give them the same consideration you give your props and costume pieces.

A good entrance establishes your character. You enter the stage bringing your whole history with you and if the audience believes, you're home free! Believe me, if you enter a space with your whole life behind you, with all that knowledge supporting you, it can be thrilling.

I say this because so often an actor will ask, "Do I enter here?" Yes. They come in the door and then they act. No! Act before you come in the door. Bring everything with you. Bring where you've been, what's happened, what's needed, what the intention is.

And when you exit, take everything that has changed by being on stage and carry that with you as you head somewhere – to your death! To your love! To the dentist!

If you exit weakly, thoughtlessly, then that will be the last thing the audience remembers until the next entrance. They will be unsure of who you are, what's going on, and you will have to work to reestablish yourself.

Think of the image you want to leave behind. The lights go out on stage and that last glimmer on the retina before the stage goes dark, that is the feeling left.

FAIRY TALES and MOTIVATION

I want you to bring a fully realized, flesh and blood character on stage with you. You need to be fully engaged before you ever enter the stage.

That's why thinking about a character's "motivation" is incredibly useful to the actor. Build up everything you need to drag some real human life onto the stage.

However, performing in many fairy tales over the years has taught me another lesson.

In fairy tales, stuff just happens. "Once upon a time there was a king and he was very angry all the time." We don't know what made him angry or when the anger started or how he feels about his anger. We just know he's angry.

What happened to Cinderella's parents? Where do Bartholomew Cubbins' hats come from? Why is Hansel and Gretel's step-mother such a witch? It doesn't matter. Some things just are.

So, while motivation is an indispensable tool for the actor, sometimes it can be very freeing and a lot of fun to just jump in and go!

LOOK FOR THE PIN

John Barrymore and Constantin Stanislavski were having dinner. Barrymore asked Stanislavski how he selected people to be in his acting company. Stanislavski said, "Leave the room, please. I will hide a pin somewhere on this table and you will look for it."

Barrymore left the room. Stanislavski hid the pin.

When Barrymore returned he looked under a plate, a saucer, a candelabra. He soon found the pin under a teacup. Stanislavski said, "You would be in my company."

"Why me?" asked Barrymore.

Stanislavski replied, "Because you simply looked for the pin and nothing else. You would be surprised how many young actors act out looking for a pin, shaking their heads, flailing their arms, instead of just looking for the pin."

Look for the pin.

DISCOVERY

Isn't it much more fun to discover a story than it is to be lectured to? This is the theater! We're explorers, inviting the audience to travel with us as we discover the world!

I've seen plays that would have been better off being a TV movie, or a lecture, or a letter to the editor. We have to demand more!

Don't you want stories that challenge you, inspire you, confront you, move you? Stories that contain within them the full scope of life and a search for meaning? The possibility, at least, for the great "aha!"

And don't let others discourage you. A critic once dismissed our production of *The 500 Hats of Bartholomew Cubbins* as "trite" and "silly." He couldn't see the profound truths that can be discovered in a simple tale.

Fairytales, parables and folktales contain whole worlds of human experience. How else could they last through the ages? They are stories of life and death, betrayal and sacrifice, growth and decay. In *Cubbins*, sometimes there are things that "just happen to happen to be." It reminds me of what John Lennon said: "life is what happens while you're busy making other plans." The critic mistook simplicity for simplistic, and so he could not allow any discovery to occur.

Discovery! Don't we all pray that we discover what turns us on? A job, a career, friends, passions, a mate, love at first sight, true faith? Don't we long to share the sense of discovery Galileo felt seeing a crater on the moon? Keep searching. Keep seeking. That is our responsibility. Seek, and you shall find.

We were rehearsing *Johnny Tremaine* (1969) and I was playing Paul Revere. One day the director said to me, "Act as if you have mouse in your pocket."

I tried really hard to imagine what it was like to walk around with a mouse in my pocket.

I was being too literal.

What the director meant was: sometimes you have a secret. Don't give away everything you've got the moment you hit the stage. Keep a little something back, some delightful little secret, and the audience will sense it. And only let it out when the time is right!

INFECTION

You are a carrier of infection.

You must allow yourself to become infected by a character. Only then can you hope to infect an audience.

This doesn't always happen. Some plays and characters are sterile. Avoid them.

OBSERVATION

I had an acting class in which the teacher asked us to observe someone and then bring back our observations to share with the class. I went to the bus depot and watched a man sitting on a bench. I watched and watched. I tried to memorize his movements. I came back to the class and did a pantomime.

The teacher said, "Jerry, you will be a good actor. You'll never be a great actor, but you'll be a good actor." I was crushed. It took me 30 years to get over that.

What I should have asked and what the so-called teacher should have explained is "WHAT IS THE POINT OF THIS!?"

As actors, we have a vague sense that we should be good observers. But why? What's the point?

It's not to become mimics. That's where I went wrong. I was merely imitating a man at a bus depot.

Instead, we observe because we need to be able to express inner lives through outer forms. Sometimes we work from the outside in, sometimes from inside out. But we need as many tools as possible to express ourselves.

When you observe someone, ask yourself a lot of questions. What am I looking at? Why is this person sitting like this? What is he waiting for? What is he afraid of? Where is she leaving from and where is she going to? Why is she doing that? Make up your answers.

Yes, make them up! You can never really know what goes through another person's mind. So you must fill in the blanks.

This is different, of course, than observing a funeral, a wedding, a fight in the bar. People behave differently in these high stress, heightened moments. I'm talking about the simple, quiet moments of day-to-day life, full of little idiosyncratic, individual moments that make us who we are. Do this for a while and you will begin to see that every moment has its own importance. Every little gesture is a part of life.

Write down what you see and your responses to what you see. You'll remember them far longer that way and it all gets filed away in the encyclopedia of your mind.

You never know when your observations will become useful. It may be weeks, or months, or years from now.

When Kathie and I were married, her father walked around the reception with a Polaroid camera around his neck, calling out as a paparazzi would. Decades later I played a character in *Rembrandt Takes a Walk* (1989) and I knew exactly what I had to do. I got a Polaroid camera, wore it around my neck, and called out as a paparazzi would at everybody. It was perfect.

What's real on stage is not the same as what's real in life. Don't get too hung up on this.

An intimate conversation between two people is full of overlapping words and sentence fragments and is probably much too quiet for anyone else to hear. But an intimate conversation between two CHARACTERS needs to be understood. The audience needs to be guided along the journey and not be confused.

If the playwright chooses to have dialogue overlap, it's just that – a choice.

And it's not just dialogue. How you move, where you look, where you stand – all this is dictated by the story you're trying to tell.

IT'S NOT REAL LIFE.

You've been cast as Juliet. Or Hamlet. Lots of terrific actors have played those parts before you, and many of their performances are available to you right on your computer. Just head to YouTube. But you say, "Oh no, I can't possibly watch any of that. I don't want to steal anything."

Let me ask you something. When a painter goes to a museum and copies the work of a master, is he stealing? Of course not. He's studying the work of artists he admires and taking from them that which means the most to him. Brush strokes, use of light, the building up of shapes, composition, line and color. How does the size of the canvas relate to the subject of the painting? This is what you're doing.

You observe the work of masters to see how they put together a performance and compare it to your own. Is your performance too big for the frame? Too small? Is there too much detail? Not enough color? It's all observation. Isn't it?

Besides, unless you're a skilled mimic, you won't be able to duplicate another actor's performance. So go ahead. Imitate artists you admire. Get it into your body. See what they do, respond honestly, take what you need, and trust that, with time, you'll make it your own.

SO MANY LIVES

I have been blessed to live many lives. I have been a curious visitor to other times, other places, to worlds that no longer exist.

I love it.

I love doing research, discovering styles, language, thoughts, feelings, philosophies, beliefs and superstitions of ages gone by.

Many, many lives.

How many have I put on like a new coat and worn for six weeks, only to discard it at the end of the run, waiting for the tailor to outfit the next one?

Here are some of them.

King Arthur	Thomas	Mr. Darling
Johnny	Diaforus	Nadd of Didd
Appleseed	Dr. Livesy	Archibald
Ali Baba	Muff Potter	Craven
Paul Revere	John Worthing	Elrond
Bob Cratchit	Fagin	Sultan
The March	Friar Laurence	Bottom
Hare	Pied Piper	Mr. Webb
Rip Van	Captain Jack	Long John
Winkle	Absolute	Silver
Lelio	Captain Hardy	Harpagon
Coviere	Wicked	White Knight
Nutcracker	Stepmother	Mark Twain
Gepetto	Pa Ingells	

Toad of Toad Hall	Old Galileo	Capulet
The Invisible Man	Afar the Angel	Professor Kirk
Scrooge	The Wizard of Oz	Rajaswami
Thorin Oakenshield	Bloodletter	Mrs. Dickens
	Yertle the Turtle	Dr. Seuss' Fish

I list these characters to show the variety of roles you could be asked to play. Isn't it thrilling to think where your career might take you? Different ages, different cultures, and so many characters within you waiting to be revealed!

MEXICANS

I'm still looking in antique shops and garage sales for a certain toy. It's a little rubber man my brother and I called "Mexican" because he came with a wide hat. The two of us had seen a movie where a Mexican was shot over and over and did not die. That's when we both decided we wanted to be Mexicans.

I have been haunted by certain characters. Fagin, Long John Silver, Bottom, among others.

When I played Fagin in *Oliver Twist* (1990), I summoned him. I would lie on my back, close my eyes, and speak to him.

There was a moment in the play where I didn't know what to do, so I asked Fagin about it. And Fagin said, "I dance."

I went to the director and told him that Fagin needed to dance at this moment. He loved the idea and we put it into the play. Fagin danced. Fagin the pimp, the robber, the thief, the killer, and it was perfect.

I summoned Fagin many times, asking his advice, and he was always willing to give it. Maybe I didn't talk to Fagin enough, because, even when the production was over, he'd come creeping out. Words of his would come out of my face, voices, rhythms, a cock of the head.

He is a dark, tortured creature and he's hungry for light. For life. My life! I wonder if he'll ever be done with me.

I think hauntings are common to many actors. When you tap into certain parts of your psyche, you're inviting all kinds of creatures to crawl into the light. Sometimes it's a revelation. Sometimes it's an infection.

But then new characters come along and, hopefully, help put to rest the uneasy spirits that have come before.

ACTING AS A JOB

I've been looking at the dictionary again. Here's what it says a job is:
 1. An action requiring some exertion, a task or undertaking
 2. An activity performed in exchange for payment, especially one performed regularly as a trade or occupation
 3. A criminal act, especially a burglary

I particularly like that last one.

But my point is, for most people, a job is something you do, then leave. But I can't leave the theater.

Certain characters follow me around. They infect my life and are with me twenty-four hours a day.

I say "enough!" I try to leave it behind. It doesn't work.

That's why I never say acting is my job. The best, most accurate thing I can say is, "I am an actor."

ACTING AND FRIENDS

He is a friend to all and a
brother to every other scout.
Boy Scout Law #4

As an actor, I have lived a very isolated life, even though I have always longed for a friend I could go for drinks with and talk to, in a very real way, about work, everything. I have been a paid actor for nearly fifty years, but I still really have no male friend, someone near to me, physically and spiritually, that I can share my triumphs and tribulations with.

There's not a lot of time for the usual relationships in the theater. You often work seven days a week, with an ever-changing schedule, from early in the morning to quite late at night. You perform for the public, then the public leaves and you're left with only the private.

Birthday parties, graduations, funerals – I've missed all of these and more, because I had to be on the stage.

I have tried to make my experience on stage extraordinary. I suppose it's only fair that "real life" will lack some things.

There is a great line from the movie *The Dresser*. Albert Finney says to the young, would-be artist, you must be willing to give up "that which we know of as life." How true.

However, what I *do* have and always have had is my wife. Without Kathie, I would have gone mentally ill years ago. How she has stood hearing all this stuff I have been lamenting about these past fifty years, I don't know.

CHILDRENS THEATRE

Why Children's Theatre? Why Theater?!

Since long before recorded history began, people have gathered around a fire, or a well, or under a sacred tree, and a storyteller would step forward and begin. Were the young ones sent away, or rather, were they a cherished part of the audience?

I look out at our audiences today and see a whole community: children, parents, grandparents, families, young adults on dates. What could be greater?

They come in, sit in the red seats, and say, "All right, take me away!" We must give them the gift they seek.

If you find yourself performing for children, you must never condescend to them. Sadly, a lot of "children's theater" does just that. But they don't want to be played down to. They want to be played up to and beyond!

Student audiences experience the play differently than their parents. For many of them, what they see happening on stage is really happening. That carries a responsibility for us to respect the power of live theater and strive to tell stories that have real weight. Nothing mindless or heartless. Conflict, yes! Drama, yes! High stakes, yes! But told with taste, artistry and vision.

They say the audience gets the show it deserves. This may or may not be true for adult audiences, but it is wrong to think this way when your audience is young. Yes, sometimes, a student audience is full of donkeys. And donkeys will be donkeys and then go home and eat some grass. But you never know if somewhere among them is a young person who wants the story you are telling. Who needs it! And will remember the experience for the rest of her life.

If the audience isn't responding the way you think they should, don't blame them. First, look at yourself. Look to the work, look to the intent, look to the vision, look to the theme. Is the story clear? Is it ambiguous? If it's ambiguous, was that intentional?

When they cough and yell and scream, don't try to rise above the noise. You couldn't anyway. Try speaking normally. Make them come to you. Don't let them take over the show. Instead, give them the show you created.

Only twice in my life have a seen a show stopped because of an unruly audience. The first was when I was a high school student. My class went to the Guthrie Theater to see a matinee of *Hamlet*. Student audiences were much less sophisticated in those days and we were particularly awful. George Grizzard, who was playing Hamlet, stopped the show, turned to the audience and told us to settle down or he would not go on. He pleaded with us, "Don't you realize how hard this is? Help me!"

Years later, as an actor in *Our Town*, I watched the Stage Manager stop the show to tell a section of the audience to be quiet. Like my high school class, these students were new to live theater. They didn't really understand that it's not like a movie. It didn't occur to them that we, on stage, hear them, see them and are affected by them.

These are the exceptions. Most of the time, school shows are my favorite to perform. The energy in the room as the lights go down is electric. They yell and shout and whistle. But then the lights come up on our story, the students settle down, and off we go!

You learn the most about your work from audiences of children. They do not stand for mediocrity. Adults will sit politely for boring shows, but students will talk, wrestle, cough and carry on. They will not be fooled by actor tricks. They know exactly what you're giving and what you're holding back.

They are also often the most generous audiences, most likely to suspend their disbelief, most likely to forgive, most likely to be infected by your work. They are the most likely to respond honestly to your work. Isn't that what you hope for?

They love to play. Don't you?

Give children the best show you can. Perform as you would for a visiting head of state.

POST-SHOW DISCUSSIONS

After school matinees we invite students to stay for a brief discussion with a few actors and a stage technician.

Usually, children raise their hands and ask how we did this or that. I'm always amazed and delighted when they ask about something that didn't happen. Or rather, it didn't happen on stage, but it certainly did happen in their minds. It's a lesson in the audience's willingness to suspend their disbelief and go on journey.

We mustn't forget that the experience of the play is brand new for these audiences. Hopefully, they've just been on a journey. What we do next is part of that and will be the last thing they remember.

That's why I don't like it when the discussion gives away all our secrets. We create magic on stage, and, like a magician, we shouldn't be in a big hurry to give away all our tricks. It makes the magic less magical.

Instead, I prefer to demonstrate something. Show off a costume in all its detail. Or pick one stage effect to demonstrate and keep the rest a mystery.

I've had children ask me where I go after the performance is over. They assume I live there at the theater, just waiting until it's time to do the show again. (This is sometimes true.) But the point is, actors are magical creatures to these audiences.

RELAXATION

"I'm so nervous," I said to my dentist. "I'm afraid about getting this crown. You're going to grind away a part of my body and replace it with something artificial."

"How can you be nervous?" my dentist asked. "You're an actor! You perform in front of thousands of people. How can this be nerve-racking?"

An interesting question.

I told him that in the theater, I know how it's all going to turn out. "In life," I said, "like in this chair, I don't know how it's going to turn out. It might not get wrapped up neatly in the final act." There is safety in the knowing.

Maybe it's the safety I've found on stage that allows me to feel more alive there than I do in my life. Perhaps it's the security that allows me to relax, to use all my senses, to listen and respond.

Directors are always telling actors to relax. Relax! You're too uptight. You're stiff. You're not listening! But how do you get to a state of relaxation on stage?

It's a very unnatural place to be. The lights, costumes, and most of all – all those people sitting in the dark, staring at you, judging you. How are you supposed to relax?

Does it come from breathing? Listening? Knowing your cues? Or is there something else at work?

Maybe we're using the wrong word. Does anyone really "relax" on stage? When I say I'm relaxed, do I really mean I'm comfortable in the knowing? That I'm secure in the choices I've made?

Is a fighter relaxed before the fight? Should he be? Maybe I should be *more* nervous!

I don't think so. Being nervous is limiting. I don't want to tense up. I prefer to think of it as being filled with "anticipation." That's more positive, right? Don't come tell me you're scared to go out on stage! You'll make me scared, too. Say, "I'm filled with anticipation!" Anticipation lets your muscles stay fluid while being filled with energy. It's good and healthy.

Be secure in your thoughts. Let yourself fill with anticipation. You are about to tell a story and you want to be in control of yourself. You want your body relaxed and responsive. And if any little flashes of inspiration occur, you'll be free to act on them.

I have seen actors do push-ups in the wings, trying to feel exhausted because their character was meant to be exhausted. I guess one does what one must, but haven't we all been exhausted? Don't you remember what that feels like?

I think being relaxed means only using the muscles that you need.

If you need to jump over a wall, jump over the wall. If you need to pick up a cup, pick up a cup.

I saw a child directed to cross the stage and pretend she was catching butterflies. She ran out, jumping up and down, making grotesque faces. She looked like she had hot coals in her pants. If she had had to speak, I think she would've choked and collapsed. Why not pretend there's a butterfly in front of you? See it in your mind's eye and try to catch it. Just concentrate on that and all the excess crap will disappear. You'll be in a relaxed state, doing the task, playing the moment, pursuing the goal and playing the intent.

Have you had the experience where you open a show and you're working yourself to death, sweating like crazy, using every muscle? Then, as the run continues, you find yourself sweating less and less. Eventually you begin using only the muscles necessary to do the given scene.

THIS IS THE KEY TO RELAXATION. ONLY USE THE MUSCLES YOU NEED!

If you can accomplish this on opening night – and I have seen it – it is a wonderful comforting energy to those around you.

MAKEUP

Holy, holy holy!

The ritual begins. You sit in front of the mirror, your face blank, expressionless. The makeup kit is placed before you, perhaps a hand towel underneath, and a box of tissues to the side. The kit opens and you know that somewhere in there is your new face, your new mask, waiting to be realized.

The base is applied, smoothed and blended. Then darkness and shadows, highlights and edges, and before you now is another you, the same you, but transformed. Final touches to the eyebrows, or a beard and glasses, or just a few dabs of clown white, complete the transformation.

This tradition, this putting on the paint, has passed through many cultures, through many centuries, and is a holy ritual. You are continuing a tradition that has been passed down since some ancient ancestor of ours first smeared blood on his face to tell his story of the hunt.

Cherish this ritual! What music is playing? What environment surrounds you?

God, I love a beard and mustache. A monocle! I love the smell of certain makeup sticks. And the sense it all gives me of play. True play. Real play. Make-believe. Transformation.

Transformation! Isn't that why we are in the theater? I love the transforming power of a new face. It affects all the rest of my character - the attitude, the way I carry my body, my costume, my words and silences.

When I first began at CTC the whole cast made up together. We sat in one long row in front of a sheet of plywood with mirrors behind it. Twenty or so people making up together.

I sat next to Karlis Ozols in my first show. He was a six foot, seven inch giant, and made up with the greatest care, artistry and finesse. That was a lesson.

In those days it was grease sticks and Texas dirt. Crepe hair was ironed on the ironing board to make mustaches and small beards. We cut the crepe hair and glued it right to our faces.

Giesen's Costume House went out of business a few years later - 1969 or 1970, maybe - and John Jenkins went to the closeout and bought a collection of wigs and facial pieces for CTC. Everyone was thrilled.

I remember the first custom-ordered pieces we had. They were hair pieces made for Bain Boehlke as Fagin in *Oliver Twist*. I remember Bain putting them on and the thrill of seeing a handmade beard and wig!

I write all of this to share with you the great sense of play we had, the joy of putting on the pieces, the sense of ritual, the respect for them. And the power they had - or that we bestowed upon them - to transform us.

I love putting on rubber noses, hairpieces, beards, disguises. I love burying myself in the character. Let me not show out, not in the least! Let me disappear and let the character come out in all his glory, his language, his physicality. How glorious to traipse around the stage in these disguises! Nothing pleases me more.

Is it because I don't like who I am? Or how I am? Or that I'm so uncomfortable with who I am that I welcome these disguises? I don't know.

But I HAVE loved it since I was a little boy. I loved Halloween, or even just playing with my brother, wearing cowboy hats and holsters. Wearing a Superman t-shirt. On "Indian Night" at Cub Scouts (that wouldn't happen anymore). Being a member of the Order of the Arrow. Dressing up for plays in the church basement, to high school shows, to college productions and to CTC.

At every moment I loved it.

Holy, holy, holy!

PROPS

The blessed props, they're called.

(I might be the only one who calls them that.)

They are essential. Look at people as they stand and talk. Watch what they do with the things around them – phones, newspapers, coffee cups, books, eyeglasses - all the idiosyncratic little interactions that we have with inanimate objects all day long.

The skillful use of props can ground the character and engage the audience because something real is happening onstage. If your character eats an apple, you, the actor, can't *pretend* to eat the apple. You either eat it or you choke. Good prop choices create a reality that is undeniable.

The right prop can make a character come alive. Mark Twain's cigar, Long John Silver's crutch, Fagin's coat pockets filled with odds and ends, watches and handkerchiefs.

Learn to love your props and use them to your best advantage. Your research will suggest props for your character. Bring rehearsal props with you early on as needed. Remember, acting is about choices. There are no bad choices, only better ones.

COSTUMES

What's true for makeup and props is true for costumes, too. I've had characters that eluded me completely until I put on the costume and suddenly, all was revealed.

Ideally, your rehearsal room will contain a rehearsal rack with appropriate bits and pieces of costumes – hats, cloaks, coats, etc., as well as props for the actors to play with.

But don't be obsessive. There is a danger in these things. Sometimes rehearsal props and costumes are given lives of their own and it becomes very hard to part with them.

Care for your costume. Cherish it. Be good to it - better than your own clothes.

I love seeing old name tags on costume pieces that were worn years earlier by another actor. It thrills me to think that some of their energy and charm lingers in the folds of this garment, especially if you know the actor.

There was a time in the history of the theater in the 1800s when the actor showed up with a travelling case inside of which were costumes of the roles they knew they could play. "I can play Laertes. Here is my costume." Talk about a long run of a show.

I am amazed at costumer designers who do not talk with actors after the show closes. Don't they want to know how the costume was to work with?

Please, costumers, talk to actors and make it a part of the ritual. When a show closes, find out about your work. You know how actors are - they will say, "oh, it was fine," but prod them. Tell them it's okay to tell the truth and discoveries will be made for everyone.

Too often the actor has been reduced to showing up, getting a fitting, asking a question or two, and taking what is given.
The actor says, "I think my character has a glorious moustache." The designer says, "you will not have a mustache, but glasses are okay."
I don't really blame actors for not speaking up. Many have been browbeaten, told over and over to be thankful that they even have a job. They are usually tight-lipped and worried about the next job offer. They don't want to burn any bridges, but what the heck, this is an art!

Can't we all just talk? Share ideas? Communicate?

I know many designers and actors would love to work more collaboratively, but are prevented by the systems we've imposed on ourselves to make things run "smoothly." To make sure we meet our deadlines. Art is dangerous and so are deadlines. Let's find the best way to present all ideas, no matter where they come from, and at least listen to them.

Yes, it's a two-way street. All of us need to be generous to each other and willing to listen.

Maybe I'm talking about the exception to the rule. But that's okay. Exceptions should be considered!

AUDIENCES

With every performance, we hope the audience will quickly form a personality – a joyful, rich, cohesive personality. One that we can play upon during the show in the way a musician plays upon a flute. One that enthusiastically helps shape the rhythm of the performance by their truthful response.

In children's theater, this is often impossible. The audience is usually a mix of children, their parents or grandparents and other adults who've come to the theater without children. Different ages respond to the play in very different ways. You'll have areas of the house that are extremely vocal and other areas that are completely silent. This isn't bad, it's just the way it is.

The only thing that really irritates me about an audience is a false response. Fake laughter, fake coughing, fake applause. I don't know why, but some audiences show up having predetermined what the show will be and that's what they see, no matter what is happening in front of their eyes.

There's something ugly about a forced "ha ha." It's brutal and disarming and useless.

If the audience only knew how important it is! They would show up and leave their baggage in the lobby and come into the house ready to suspend their disbelief. Please, audiences, come to us willing to travel on a journey. Laugh, cry, shout, stomp your feet and do what you will! Good or bad, I don't care, just give me a true response.

That is what feeds the actor.

It's the audience more than anything that guarantees that no performance will ever be exactly the same as another. Isn't that the most exciting aspect of it? Constantly changing yet remaining basically the same? That's a lot like life, isn't it?

LAUGHTER

I remember particular laughs. When I was in one act play and the audience roared. I felt like an actor!

It was *Bellavita*, a one-act by Pirandello. I played a slick lawyer named Mr. Contento. My wife held a puppy in her arm while she vacuumed the stage. Guy Paul played a poor man who appeared on my doorstep. I put out my hand to shake his. He collapsed. I looked at my hand. I looked at the audience. It killed.

These were laughs in which I felt completely in control. Sometimes it can feel as if the audience has you running around the stage pushing a ball. It's far better to feel that you are in control, crafting the moment, playing upon the audience like a musician plays an instrument.

I love it.

The audience's laughter is the best medicine I have ever taken. It's like a full meal with chocolate and dessert. It's invigorating. Inoculating.

And as their laughter inoculates you, you infect the audience. You infect them with a little bit of your soul. It becomes contagious and spreads through the whole auditorium. The result is a oneness, a singularity of people together, like a ship traveling in one direction. Hopefully they don't bail out.

CURTAIN CALLS

Do not be embarrassed by the curtain call.

You have made the journey, and this is the time to tie the knot and put the dot at the end of the sentence. The *finis*.

Curtain calls are important because your mind wants a release from the character's consciousness and to put away their emotions.

Take your moment. Enjoy the warmth. You have told a story.

THE BLESSED THEATER

It is said that being in a play is like being in a small car crash, it takes that much out of you. But it is oh, so cleansing. It's therapeutic, this exploration of your feelings. The theater reminds me that I am alive!

When I have been numbed by TV and newspapers, bombarded by press, commercials, advertisements and solicitations to the point where I want to withdraw, the blessed theater refreshes me and heals and focuses me.

The play has opened. You have several weeks, or months, of performances to go. You know every performance is important, but the energy of opening night has begun to fade. What do you do?

You must learn how to grow in the part. But you must grow constructively. Not in a way that exaggerates or embellishes, but in a way that deepens the performance and keeps it fresh.

We were doing our production of *A Christmas Carol* (1969), adapted by Fred Gaines. I was playing Bob Cratchit and as the run continued, I kept finding new things to do. I thought I was making exciting discoveries. After a while, Bain, who was playing Scrooge, called me over. "What are you doing?" he asked. "You're not supporting me. You're not supporting yourself. You're not supporting the play. This is all just distraction. You had a lovely character in Bob, but now this – this has nothing to do with anything."

That was a lesson.

It can be difficult to feel the difference between growing creatively and growing distractively. But you must try.

Give yourself an objective. One tool I use is to set a task for a performance. "Today I will listen, listen as closely as I can. That is my task." Other days I say, "Today I will observe as never before."

No matter how long the run, there are still discoveries to be made. Focus on the performance in a new way. Reread the script. Watch the show again from the wings.

If you are a young actor, the quickest way to establish your own aesthetic and refine your own technique is by the proper observation of the actors around you. Learn from the ones who have something to teach you. Avoid the ones who have nothing to offer.

Away from the theater, a long run is a great time to take care of yourself in other ways. Walk, exercise and eat well. Give up something undesirable. Take on something you have thought about but never done. Explore all of yourself, hobbies and interests, drawing, music, painting or baking bread.

By nurturing the creative impulses in other parts of your life, you can't help but make yourself a better actor. You're exercising the parts of your mind where creativity lives.

Some characters and some shows just don't come together.

I don't know what the problem was, but the director of *Harriet the Spy* and I never connected.

In rehearsal one day, two actors were playing a romantic scene on a park bench. I decided to add a little atmosphere by whistling some bird songs. My old director would have loved that. This director turned to where I was sitting at the back of the room and angrily snapped her fingers at me to get me stop. So much for making a small contribution to rehearsal.

In one scene, my character played the saxophone. Having played clarinet for a dozen years, I started working on the saxophone so that I could play it for real on stage. The director said, no, "We're using a recording of John Coltrane instead." I was dismayed that our ideas about the sophistication of the playing were so very different.

In another scene, I was on a high set piece. One day during the scene change, the stage tech pushed the piece so hard that it fell over and I crashed to the floor. Helplessly crashing to the floor – that's pretty much how I felt about the whole experience.

Maybe I should have asked more questions. Maybe I should have turned off my artistic juices in the rehearsal process and looked to performances for inspiration. I don't know.

Sometimes this just happens.

But you keep going. You remind yourself that you're not alone. You are part of a community of artists and you're doing the best you can. You keep working.

Keep the faith!

TOAD OF TOAD HALL

Sometimes everything comes together very quickly.

In *Wind in the Willows* (1995), adapted for the stage by Tom Olson, I played Toad of Toad Hall.

The first thing I did was rent the Disney video. It's a short piece – about twenty minutes – and I think John Mills provides the voice of Toady. There was a moment when Toad goes flying off his gypsy caravan with a certain look in his eye. In that moment, I knew just how to play him.

Toady gives his full concentration to whatever is immediately before him. Then that's forgotten and the next thing gets his full attention. Then the next. Kenneth Grahame describes him as "restless."

He experiences everything deeply – the pride of wealth, the despair of prison, the thrill of escape, the joy of the open road, the fear of battle, the triumph of victory, the satisfaction of false modesty. He's a very "human" toad.

I knew the costume would make a big difference to Toady's physicality so I went to the costume designer, Bill Schroeder. Bill's costume design was terrific. He gave Toady a huge tummy and big glasses for the eyes. After seeing the design I brought a bathing cap and goggles to rehearsal so I could immediately start trying them out.

Toady's spirit is so important. He loves life. He loves adventure. He loves to play! So do I! Maybe that's why I took to him so quickly. Also, I went through fifteen years in which I owned twenty-five cars, so I know something about the madness of desire for the motorcar.

I attacked rehearsals with total abandon. I gave Toady the freedom to do whatever he wished. We were shaping scenes right up until opening. It took a few weeks of performances for me to fully relax into the role, but from the first school shows – traditionally our toughest audiences – the students were very responsive to the play and Toady in particular.

With *Harriet the Spy*, I never figured out what the production was or how I fit into it. Sometimes that happens. With *Wind in the Willows*, I knew how to play Toady from the first read-through. Sometimes that happens, too.

PLAY SELECTION

I am amazed at those who suggest plays for a season because they think those titles will make a lot of money. "People will flock to this!" Maybe not. If you knew what people wanted wouldn't you make a million dollars on the stock market? Human beings are a puzzle. As the FBI agent said about bank robbers, "Who knows what they'll do next?"

Instead of trying to predict the biggest money-maker, why not select a season based on synchronicity, or serendipity, or grace, or whatever you want to call it?

Directors: select any season of plays you want, as long as you have some sort of vision for them, some sort of creative impulse that makes these plays the ones we have to do.

Maybe it was something you've read, something you've talked about, an unexpected eye twinkle, something that makes you say, yes! I'm interested in working on this. Maybe it comes from listening to your actors and choosing something that helps them grow. Maybe it's a story that has always fascinated you, or a theme you feel needs exploring. Maybe it's a work that has always been a mystery to you. Maybe it's a reaction to your community, your organization, your playwright friend, ANYTHING, as long as it's a TRUE FEELING.

That's what actors are looking for.

Have faith that what you want to do is what you should be doing.

CRITICS

I've kept a review of *Rip Van Winkle* (1970) in which the critic said the one thing missing from the production was Bain Boehlke in the title role. I was playing Rip Van Winkle. That one hurt.

I've had reviews that brought me to my knees, weeping. I've had reviews that left me bewildered at not being mentioned. I've had glowing reviews that made me proud, and poor reviews that felt like someone picking at an open sore.

Some actors say they never read reviews. They must be very secure in their work. Or they're liars.

I keep all my reviews. Why? I suppose it has something to do with the ephemeral nature of theater. Sometimes, later, I wonder if a show even happened. A review, good or bad, is proof it did.

Actors dismiss reviews, saying, "It's just one person's opinion." Yes, but, oh, how much weight we give to that one person! We make the critics whatever they are to us: angels, devils, blessings from above, ignoramuses, snobs, idiots.

With children's theater, I think the critics are often at a loss. Many of our plays are new plays. The critics have nothing to compare it to. My performance as the father in *Beauty and the Beast* can't be judged against another's performance because it doesn't exist. This makes critics nervous.

And many critics come in with an idea of what "theater for children" is, or can be, or should be, and this prevents them from seeing what it really is. They don't see how difficult the work is. They don't see the breadth and scope of what children's theater tries to be. We tell stories of love and hate and forgiveness and redemption. They see "a kid's show."

A final note about the critics. When Richard Burton was asked about reviews, he said, "Why should I read them? If they are bad, who wants to see them? And if they are good, they are never good enough!"

THE EXTRAORDINARY

Movies and television have cameras that can get very close and explore the minutiae of daily life.

We don't. The audience is too far away for that.

We don't go to the theater to see a person going to the bathroom. We want to see what happens when you lift the toilet lid and a rat jumps out and bites at you! (That happened to a friend of mine.)

The theater should be an extraordinary place. We need to tell extraordinary stories, full of extraordinary characters doing extraordinary things.

This can be scary, especially for young actors. They struggle against it and fight to make the extraordinary, ordinary. But don't be scared. Welcome it. Welcome powerful emotions and extraordinary situations. The theater can be a great art and a joy to perform, but you have to be willing to embrace it.

COMEDY and TRAGEDY

Because a play has a happy ending doesn't mean it's simple-minded or all bubblegum and sunshine. It can be messy, dark and dangerous. But at the end, the protagonist achieves some kind of success.

That's the promise of comedy. Mistakes are made, but we learn from them. People are hurt, but they forgive. Lovers are reunited. The villain is punished.

Laughter for me is the great elixir. It refreshes me. It's a transfusion for the soul.

Of course, tragedy has its own rewards. You go through the journey with an audience and together you travel somewhere you've never been before. It's like running a race. And once I've made it to the finish line, I feel spent, but cleansed.

It's interesting to me that one person's comedy can be another person's tragedy. At the end of *The Little Match Girl*, the spirit of the little girl ascends to heaven, but the body of the little girl has frozen to death. Some grownups thought this show was too dark for children's theater. But they didn't see the same show their children saw. The adults saw death. Their children saw hope. Hope that things like that can be prevented. Young people have so much hope!

When my son Bobby was a boy, he played a small role in the theater's production of *Cinderella*. It was his job to make sure the clock struck midnight. An important job! After doing that, he would creep down into the orchestra pit and sit next to the percussionist, Jay Johnson.

That Christmas, Bobby asked for a set of drums. I went to Jay and he helped me put together a drum kit for Bobby. We set it up in the basement. Five years later, Bobby came up out of the basement, climbed into a van, and drove to Seattle. Now he's the drummer in a rock band.

All the arts are related. They all take discipline. They all take commitment. You learn to take direction. You learn what it's like to work toward a goal that is greater than yourself.

Give yourself over to one art and it will open doors to all the others. I am taking a drawing course and as I move my pencil across the page, using light and shadow to create contrast, I see how similar it is to acting – using laughter and danger to create contrast.

Dynamics! Without dynamics a drawing is boring. It has no personality. The same is true for a piece of music or a performance by an actor.

People are surprised when they find out movie stars are painters. "Oh, look! Anthony Quinn not only acts, he paints! Roddy McDowell is a terrific photographer!" Of course he is. It's only natural that a commitment to one art makes the other arts more accessible.

We are all artists. We are all creators.

So dabble in this and that. Whatever interests you is what you should explore. All of it will make you a better actor and maybe open doors you never knew existed.

You cannot know ahead of time what the doors may reveal! My daughter Kelly was in her first play at six months old. When she was four, she performed in a Christmas carol as the youngest daughter to my Bob Cratchit. A few years later, she went to Washington D.C to perform at Lincoln Center. But Kelly didn't grow up to become an actor. Instead, she works for a large hospital, coordinating diverse groups of people, putting together special events for the community. I've no doubt her experience in theater introduced her to many of the skills she uses every day.

My youngest daughter, Krissy, was in four productions as a child. But she was always more interested in what went on behind the scenes, the making of the production. As a school project, she photographed me putting on my makeup and costume as the White Knight in *Alice's Adventures in Wonderland*. She wanted to document the transformation from actor to character. She has gone on to become a marvelous story-teller, using video and still photography.

Whether they know it or not, this is why parents take their kids to ballet lessons, piano lessons, hip hop lessons, whatever. Those kids may grow up to be anything – astronauts, botanists, teachers, engineers or doctors. But, I believe, they will grow up to be more well-rounded individuals. They will be inoculated against meager personalities.

With the loving, positive example of teachers and artists, they will have learned about devotion, about commitment, truth, self-awareness, joyfulness, sacred spaces and ritual.

IS THEATER A DYING ART?

This is something I've thought about a lot.

My short answer is "no."

For the long answer, first we need to be clear about what we mean by "theater."

Is theater a big building with hundreds and seats, beautiful sets and fancy costumes? Of course not. Individual theaters die all the time. A theater is born, full of energy and ideas and ambition. It achieves a certain level of success. Perhaps it becomes an esteemed institution. Eventually, inevitably, it runs out of ideas and energy and then it's time to pull the plug. Good.

But what is theater? Is it storytelling? If so, we have to ask, "are stories dying?" Certainly not. We're surrounded by more stories than ever – movies, documentaries, TV shows, web series, on line, on demand, anywhere, any time.

But what about theater? What do we offer that can't be replaced by an iPad?

I think it has something to do with the energy and immediacy of live performance. That's what attracts me to the theater. We offer things you can't get from a movie screen, TV screen, or computer screen.

Audience and actor are together in the same place at the same time. This satisfies something that is deeply human and ancient. Long before human history began, our ancestors gathered around the fire to tell each other stories.

We're social animals. We need community.

As more and more of the world comes to us through screens, it becomes more and more important to find those places we come together and renew the connections we share with our fellow human beings.

I love film, but it's not the same experience. Even on opening day of a brand new movie, what you're seeing is in the past. The actors have moved on, the editors have done their job, the director is on vacation. Nothing you do as an audience member has the least effect on the film before you.

In the theater, the audience is intimately involved in the telling of the story. Every performance is different because every audience is different. Encouraging the actors, influencing the rhythm of the show, being teased and rewarded as the story unfolds.

Audiences are aware of this. Of course, not every audience *member* is. I've seen plenty of dead eyes staring back at me from the dark. And, unlike a movie that plays to millions, we play to just 500 people. Or 50. Or five. But if just one connection is made – one real, deep, human connection – isn't that enough?

Still, we in the theater lament that theater isn't what it used to be. "Where are the Shakespeares of today?" we cry. But we forget that Shakespeare wouldn't have existed without Shakespeare's audience. Audiences change, and as they change they get the theater they ask for.

Shakespeare's theater was "the Globe" and his audience got the world! Presented to them in all its wonder and wretchedness.

Our society is radically different than the one those Elizabethans experienced. We are much more diverse – good! – and our stories have become much more diverse. Good! But that makes it unlikely that one play or one playwright will speak to us the way Shakespeare spoke to his contemporaries.

As entertainment diversifies, becoming more and more targeted to specific audiences who have more and more control over the types of stories they see, it's the theater that provides something you can't get with the click of a mouse.

When I was young, I was taught to think of America as a melting pot. Now I think we're a salad bowl – lots of different ingredients, each maintaining their unique characteristics, all tossed together to create a crunchy whole.

So, while we must demand stories that reflect all people, all our neighbors, and all our different cultures, our different experiences, our different customs, our different challenges and different ways of interacting with the world, we must also celebrate those things that unite us.

This is where theater is vital.

At the heart of theater is an often unspoken recognition of the universality of human experience. We understand, without realizing it, that underneath whatever makes us uniquely different, is a deep well of something that makes us all the same.

Without this understanding, I couldn't do my job. I've never been a toad or a king or a pirate or a pickpocket, but I can play a toad or a king or a pirate or a pickpocket because I know what it's like to be alive. Audiences accept me in those roles because they know it, too. You can go anywhere, any when, to worlds that no longer exist or maybe never existed except in the imagination, and still, people laugh and cry and rage and mourn and scheme and lust and regret and reconcile. The specific, individual reasons for any of those actions will be different for each of us, but the emotional reactions themselves are universal and eternal.

Sharing that, right here, right now, is what makes the theater unique and keeps it alive. I love it. I feel more alive on stage than anywhere else. And that's what I hope to share with an audience, acting as a conduit between the story and their own immediate, living experience of it.

I have no idea what the theater will look like in a hundred years, but I'm pretty sure it will be here. And I know the elements you will find there: audience and actors, sharing the same place, in the same moment, sharing the same feelings. Sharing in the mystery of life. We need the mystery of life. We need to embrace the mystery of being alive. Not everything will be explained. But we can share that mystery with each other in the presence of holiness. We can share the holiness of community in creativity.

Yes. The holiness of community in creativity.

WHY AREN'T THERE ANY PICTURES IN THIS BOOK?

When I was performing in *A Very Old Man with Enormous Wings* (2002) playing Afar, the Angel, I had no dialogue. The character was all physical and emotional. I would go to the director, Graciela Daniele, and say, "Maybe in this scene I could make this sound." "No," she said. Later, I said, "Maybe in this scene I could say..." "No," she said. She finally came to me and said, "As soon as you spoke you would limit Afar's relationship with the audience. Let them imagine this. Don't let your character be limited." A real lesson.

I think this applies to this book. Photographs might limit your relationship to the words. This is a journey, created for you. Not for me.

A WORD OF WARNING

As you pursue your career in the theatre you will eventually meet an older actor, who will tell you about life in the theatre as he has experienced it. He will tell you about your work and about his rules of the theatre. Please, forget this actor.

Remember that with everything that is expressed, the opposite may also be true.

ACKNOWLEDGEMENTS

To the three CTC Artistic Directors and the Artistic Associates I am truly grateful. They have allowed me to have a career in the world that I love. I am also indebted to john Middleton, my friend for almost 30 years, who collaborated on editing of this book. Without John and my daughter Kelly this book would not exist. I am also grateful for the opportunities I have had to perform with so many wonderful artists, young and old, who inspired me to keep journals of the plays that made this book possible. Thank you all!

GERALD DRAKE began his professional career at the Children's Theatre Company in 1966. In those days, all the actors in the small company did more than act. Gerald was the ticket office manager, Wendy Lehr was secretary, Bain Boehlke made props, Karlis Ozols was the technical director, Frank McGovern was the stage manager, and Barbara Tyirin was the costumer and the only one who did not act, but made every costume.

Eventually Gerald was made General Office Manager, and the General Manager when the new theater opened in 1974. Gerald left the administration and was an actor/teacher. In 1979, he and Bain Boehlke took a leave of absence and produced a feature length documentary on Dietrich Bonhoeffer which won a CINE Golden Eagle Award in 1982, category of History.
Gerald returned to CTC in 1984 and received a McKnight Theater Artist Fellowship in 1999. In 2010, the mayor of Minneapolis declared September 17th, "Gerald Drake Day" in the city of Minneapolis.

He has been married for 50 years to the artist Kathie Drake and has three children, Kelly, Kristina and Bobby, and welcomes grandson Leo, a new audience member.

Made in the USA
Columbia, SC
16 August 2018